Милий Балакирев   Mily Balakirev
(1837–1910)

ПОЛНОЕ СОБРАНИЕ СОЧИНЕНИЙ

Complete Works · Sämtliche Werke
Œuvres complètes

для фортепиано
for piano · für Klavier · pour piano

V

Urtext

Редакция · Edited by · Herausgegeben von · Edité par
Konstantin Titarenko
K 253
Könemann Music Budapest

INDEX

Соната **4**
Sonata

Новеллетта **54**
Novellette

Вальс №7 . . . . **66**
Valse No.7

Пряха **83**
The Spinner – Die Spinnerin – La Fileuse

Седьмая Мазурка **91**
7-ème Mazurka

Экспромт на темы двух прелюдий Ф. Шопена **102**
Impromptu sur des thêmes de deux préludes de Fr. Chopin

APPENDIX
Сонатина **112**
Sonatina

Notes **122**

Соната   Sonata

À Serge Liapounow

I

Cadenza

L'istesso tempo

poco a poco string.

II
Mazurka

poco allargando   a tempo

18

III
Intermezzo

IV
Finale

Allegro non troppo, ma con fuoco ♩ = 132

poco a poco agitato

poco a poco cresc.

44

12 сентября 1905 г.

Новеллетта　　　Novellette

À Monsieur Constantin Tchernow

1906

Гатчина. 21 февраля 1906 г.

Вальс №7   Valse No.7

À Madame Marie Lavrova née Pogrebova

1906

K 253

68

Coda

Poco più agitato

poco a poco accel.

poco a poco cresc.

Гатчина. 8 июля 1906 г.

82

Пряха　　　La Fileuse

The Spinner - Die Spinnerin

À Monsieur Maurice Rosenthal

Allegro con fuoco　　　　　　　　　　　　　　　　　　　　　　　1906

84

poco a poco agitato

Гатчина. 2 августа 1906 г.

Седьмая Мазурка

7-ème Mazurka

À Monsieur M.D.Calvacoressi

94

96

a tempo poco meno

poco a poco ritard. al fine

Гатчина, 24/VIII 1906 г.

Экспромт
на темы двух прелюдий Ф.Шопена

Impromptu
sur des thêmes de deux préludes de Fr.Chopin

À Monsieur B.L.Zhilinsky

1907

Agitato vivace

L'istesso tempo

p amoroso

poco ritardando

108

Ossia:

1907 г.

APPENDIX

Сонатина   Sonatina

À Madame Sophie Stratonowicz

I

Allegro moderato

II

L'istesso tempo

attacca subito

III

Poco a poco più agitato

25 сентября 1909 г.

Notes

The present edition contains complete works for piano by M.A. Balakirev in 5 volumes. The works are arranged in chronological order. The fifth volume contains compositions by Balakirev written in 1905–1909. The present edition is based on the autograph manuscript and/or first edition(s) of the works. Other early editions have also been consulted, whenever justified. Evident slips of pen and printing errors have been tacitly corrected. Editorial additions reduced to a minimum appear in square brackets. The composer's peculiarities of notation and original fingering are maintained throughout. All dates are in the Old style.
In this volume the J. Zimmermann edition (proof-read and approved by the author) has been followed.

Sonata
Autograph: RNL, estate 41, No.184.
First edition: J. Zimmermann (St. Petersburg, 1905).

Andantino
Bar 1, the autograph has the marking of the metronom: ♪ = 120.

Bar 41, *cresc.* missing in the autograph.

Bar 45, *f* in the autograph.

Bar 140, *f* missing in the autograph.

Bar 154, lower stave, 4th semiquaver *f¹* in the autograph.

Intermezzo
Bar 1, the autograph has the marking of the metronom: ♪. =112.

Finale
Bar 26, lower stave, last quaver in the autograph:

Bar 84, 2nd beat in the autograph:

Bar 107, lower stave, 3rd note *c¹* in the autograph.

Bars 173-175, lower stave, in the autograph:

Bar 275, *pesante* missing in the autograph.

Bar 297, in the autograph:

Bars 363-370, lower stave, in the autograph:

Bar 419, *pesante* missing in the autograph.

Bars 435-438, lower stave, in the autograph:

Bar 447, upper stave, in the autograph:

Bars 453-469 missing in the autograph, where the ending is also different (without the marking *Poco meno mosso*):

Novellette
Autograph: RNL, estate 41, No.169.
First edition: J. Zimmermann (St. Petersburg, 1906).

Bars 148-150 in the autograph:

Bars 231-232, lower stave, in the autograph:

Valse No.7
Autograph: RNL, estate 41, No.137.
First edition: J. Zimmermann (St. Petersburg, 1906).

Bar 445, the word *Coda* missing in the autograph.

The Spinner
Autograph: RNL, estate 41, No.176.
First edition: J. Zimmermann (St. Petersburg, 1906).

Seventh Mazurka
Autograph: RNL, estate 41, No.187.
First edition: J. Zimmermann (St. Petersburg, 1906).

Bar 189, the autograph has:

Bar 273, lower stave, 2nd beat: *D flat* in the autograph.

Impromptu
Autograph: RNL, estate 41, No.374.
First edition: J. Zimmermann (St. Petersburg, 1907).

The autograph followed here. The first edition was published with a dedication *A Monsieur Ferruccio Busoni*. Busoni never answered or performed this Impromptu. In the following edition Balakirev deleted the dedication and rededicated this Impromptu to his student, the pianist B.L. Zhilinsky.

Sonatina
Autograph: RNL, estate 41, No.201.
First edition: J. Zimmermann (St. Petersburg, 1910).

This composition was published after the death of the author. The title in the first edition was *Esquisses*. Our title follows the autograph.

III (Coda)
Bars 14-15, upper stave, in the autograph:

ABBREVIATION

RNL   Russian National Library (St. Petersburg)

In 1852 a fifteen year old young gentleman got onto the conductor's podium for the first time in his life. The orchestra belonged to a Russian nobleman Oulibishev (author of a famous book on Mozart) – former diplomat, writer, a great connoisseur of music and patron of the arts. The young gentleman was Mily Balakirev.

Born in Nizhny Novgorod on January 2, 1837 into a family of a poor clerk, Balakirev received his first introduction into the world of music from his mother. He was only 10 when his mother took him to Moscow to take piano lessons from the famous piano teacher Alexander Dubuque. But the family finances did not allow for them to stay in Moscow, and they were forced to return to Nizhny Novgorod.

Nizhny Novgorod was a provincial city at that time, and not a centre of cultural life. The local theatre orchestra was conducted by Carl Eisrich – a graduate of the Vienna Conservatory and a rather mediocre musician. The performances were boring and sometimes even dreadful. Nevertheless, Eisrich could see the great talent of young Balakirev and offered to give him piano lessons free of charge. But it was Oulibishev who got Balakirev acquainted with the finest musical compositions. There at Oulibishev's estate Balakirev listened to Mozart's "Requiem", and Beethoven's symphonies. He had access to the vast library of the estate. In partnership with Oulibishev who played violin, and the estate orchestra, Balakirev frequently gave performances at domestic concerts.

In 1855 Oulibishev brought Balakirev to St. Petersburg and introduced him to Glinka. This event became a turning point in the life of the beginner composer. Encouraged and supported by Glinka, Balakirev made his public debut on February 24, 1856 performing a movement from his piano concerto. His success was overwhelming.

Balakirev moved to St. Petersburg and worked intensively on composition. "Overture on Russian Themes" was presented in 1859. During his early years in St. Petersburg Balakirev composed many romances, overtures, and music for Shakespere's "King Lear".

By the end of the 50-s the need to create a professional music school in Russia became obvious. In 1862 Anton Rubinstein founded the St. Petersburg Conservatory. The same year Balakirev together with Lomakin, an outstanding choir conductor, opened their own independent "free" school for music. Under the great influence of developing Slavophile tendencies Balakirev tried to build his school in opposition to the European ideas of musical education, presented by the Conservatory. At the same time he became interested in collecting Russian folksongs. He selected, harmonized and published a great number of these songs in 1866.

On April 18. 1865 his "Second Overture on Russian Themes" was presented at a concert in the school. This overture was published as "One Thousand Years" to commemorate the national millennium (revised in 1882, it was renamed "Russia").

In the summer of 1866 Balakirev participated in a production of Glinka "A life for the Tsar" and "Ruslan and Lyudmila" in Prague. There he befriended several Czech musicians and invited them to present their works in St. Petersburg. The Slavic concert took place at Balakirev's school on May 24. 1867. Besides Czech and Slavic music, works by Balakirev, Borodin, Cui, Musorgsky and Rimsky-Korsakov were presented. This event led Stassov to describe the new Russian composers as "The Mighty Handful" or "Mighty Five", which went down in history as a descriptive phrase.

Brilliant pianist and conductor, outstanding composer, Balakirev was regarded as a mentor by Borodin, Musorgsky and others. But as a teacher Balakirev was despotic and tyrannical. He demanded that his ideas in composition should be strictly followed; this led to a slow process of alienation of the members of the "Mighty Handful". His middle life was entirely unproductive, and only in 1894, after almost 30 years of silence did Balakirev's music start to be heard again. But the momentum was lost.

His piano concertos, composed from the 1850-s, could have been the first major Russian works, but completed 30-40 years later, they were published after Tchaikovsky's symphonies and piano concertos, Borodin's symphonies and compositions by Rachmaninov and Skryabin, and did not cause a stir in the musical community, even being left almost unnoticed.

Balakirev – a composer of outstanding abilities, but limited by his personality, never opened up his talent completely. Isolation from his colleagues and unrecognition in his later years led to the tragedy of his life.

He died at the age of 73 in St. Petersburg on May 29. 1910.

© 1998 for this edition by Könemann Music Budapest Kft.
H-1093 Budapest, Közraktár utca 10.

K 253

Distributed worldwide by
Könemann Verlagsgesellschaft mbH, Bonner Str. 126.
D-50968 Köln

Responsible co-editor: Vladimir Ryabov
Production: Detlev Schaper
Cover design: Peter Feierabend
Technical editor: Dezső Varga

Engraved in Moscow, Russia

Printed by Kossuth Printing House Co., Budapest
Printed in Hungary

ISBN 963 9059 63 3

KÖNEMANN MUSIC BUDAPEST
März 1998

PÄDAGOGISCHE AUSGABEN
für Klavier
PEDAGOGICAL EDITIONS
for piano

Pekka Vapaavuori–Hannele Hynninen:

Der Barockpianist – *The Baroque Pianist*

PIANO STEP BY STEP

Alte Tänze – *Early Dances*
Beethoven: 47 Piano Pieces
Einführung in das polyphone Spiel –
   Introduction to Polyphonic Playing
Erste Konzertstücke I–II–III–IV –
   First Concert Pieces I–II–III–IV
Etüden
Haydn: 23 Piano Pieces
Mozart: 44 Piano Pieces
Sonatinen I–II
Vierhändige Klaviermusik – *Works for
   Piano Duet* I–II

IN VORBEREITUNG – *IN PREPARATION*
Sonatinen III

FAVOURITE PIANO STUDIES

Karl Czerny:

100 Übungsstücke – *100 Exercises,*
   Op. 139
Die Schule der Geläufigkeit – *The
   School of Velocity,* Op. 299
Kunst der Fingerfertigkeit – *The Art of
   Finger Dexterity* I–II, Op. 740

FAVOURITES for piano

American Classical Songs I–II
Favourite Piano Classics I–II
Favourite Opera Classics I–II (Mozart)
Favourite Opera Classics III–IV (Verdi)
Scott Joplin: Ragtimes
Spirituals
Johann Strauss: Walzer

IN VORBEREITUNG – *IN PREPARATION*
Favourite Piano Classics III–IV
100 deutsche Kinderlieder

KLAVIERAUSZÜGE
VOCAL SCORES

Johann Sebastian Bach:
Johannes-Passion
Matthäus-Passion
Weihnachts-Oratorium

Georg Friedrich Händel:
Der Messias

Wolfgang Amadeus Mozart:
Requiem

IN VORBEREITUNG – *IN PREPARATION*
Johann Sebastian Bach:
Magnificat

KAMMERMUSIK
CHAMBER MUSIC

Violin Meets Piano I–II
Cello Meets Piano I–II

IN VORBEREITUNG – *IN PREPARATION*
Flute Meets Piano I–II